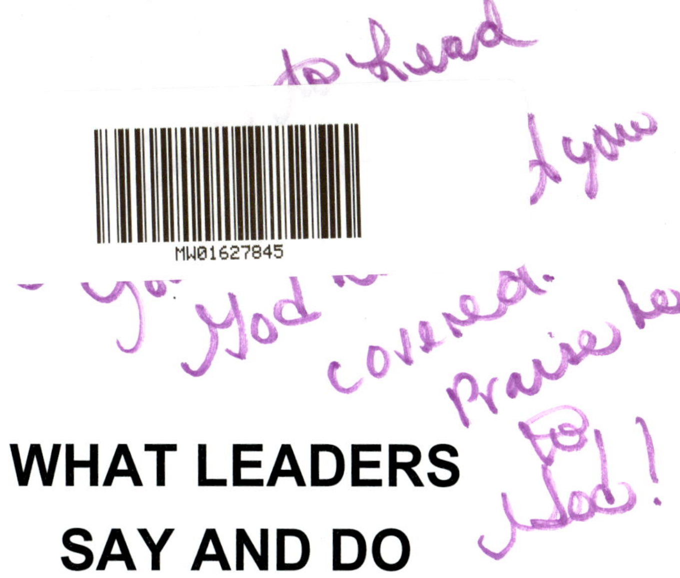

WHAT LEADERS SAY AND DO

How to Inspire Your Tribe

Ilka V. Chavez

10/21/17
To: Apostle Eric Muller, Jr.

"Lead Your Best Life Ever"

"Learn it. Live it. Lead it."
Love

What Leaders Say and Do: How to inspire your tribe

ISBN978-0-9992765-0-1

Printed in the USA

"If your actions create a legacy that inspires others to dream more, learn more, do more and become more, then, you are an excellent leader."

– Dolly Parton

Dedication

Proverbs 22:6 (NIV)
"Start children off on the way they should go, and even when they are old they will not turn from it."

I dedicate this book to my two children, Gabrielle F. Chavez and Rodolfo A. Chavez, Jr. They inspire me daily to be a great leader, to lead from within, to lead from where I am. They love me just the way I am. I learned to love myself the way I am from them—my fruits. I have many role models who not only taught me but showed me how to be a great leader, primarily my parents Herrieth L. Wilson and Alfonso Wilson (deceased). They were by no means perfect as perfection does not exist; but they led with dignity, integrity, respect, love, and strong faith.

Leaders are all around us and we are introduced to them early in our lives. Leaders come in all shapes and sizes. Some of the best leaders I have come across while growing up have been stay-at-home moms and housewives who both worked and led their households. They all led their households with pride, anchored in integrity, values, God's word and of course love for their families, their work, and their communities. Other strong leaders I have observed were fathers who worked very hard to sustain their families and who taught me the importance of discipline, self-respect, and how to mirror what you want others to learn. These men also relied heavily on God's word daily to serve as their compass to sustain and lead their families. Because these teachings were instilled in me early, I can pass this on to my children and to those I lead in the community and in the workplace.

I pray that the information I offer in this book anchors not only my children, to whom this book is dedicated, but that it also anchors leaders across the globe. My hope is that my experiences will lead readers to better understand leadership and inspire them to lead with respect, integrity, generosity, humility, trust, and in service to their tribe.

Acknowledgements

As you will read in this book, you need a tribe to accomplish almost everything in life. This book is no exception. There are so many people to thank for helping me create this book and for traveling this journey with me.

First of all, I thank God for guiding me and giving me the strength, his strength, to persevere in completing this book. All this while working full-time and building a business.

Faith, God's strength, and a very large tribe got me through this phase of my journey. They are many to thank: my family who stood in the gap for me as I spent countless hours writing and re-writing, hours sleeping off schedule and they helped cover many of my day-to-day responsibilities like walking our family dog, Samson. My mother, Herrieth, daughter, Gabrielle, and son, Rodolfo Chavez, Jr., who simply were available to do whatever I needed including periodic hugs to keep me going.

I send my deep and heartfelt gratitude to my dear friend Jan Fraser Coles, who patiently unveiled my abilities as a writer and public speaker. Her faith and discernment also helped birth this book. My editor, Helena Tavares Kennedy of htkmarketingservices.com, who I met just a few short weeks before releasing the book. She was truly a gift from God. Alberto from Zen Advertising in Peru, who has never met me in person and has been able to nail all the designs I have ordered from him including this book cover.

LAMGO marketing in Panama, Juan Caballero and Ezequiel Rodriguez, who truly believed in me and my abilities and have done nothing but work above the call of duty, including the launch of this book. My special thanks to Evolution Printing, Inc. for taking on the last-minute job to print my first batch of books.

To my cousin and agent, Ultiminio Castro Ramos - what can I say when someone sees so much potential in you and throws all his skills, knowledge and abilities and much sweat into launching this book? So much gratitude to Ultiminio for his professionalism and passion to launch what he envisioned. He led the entire effort to launch "Ilka V. Chavez" Latino America. Gracias! I also thank your wife, Indyra Saavedra de Ramos, and sons, Caleb and Marcos, for the time you took away from them to help me with so many details needed to present this book in both Spanish and English. I am grateful to you.

To my tribe, always first in my heart, you took time out to quickly review, offer edits and a suggestion to make this book what it is today. You all rock and as you know will always be part of my tribe. For those who know you are in my tribe and were not mentioned individually, you know I have nothing but gratitude and love for each of you.

Thank you Gabrielle F. Chavez (my daughter) for being my V.P. of Corporate GOLD, LLC and being available to do all tasks as assigned. My son RJ, who provided solid input on several products—I appreciate you. To Rachel Winchester, who is my right hand, office manager, and has been completely available to me to assist in the operation of my business and during this book writing journey. To Lastenia Worrell, who took time out of her school and childrearing responsibilities to help her Aunt.

A heartfelt thanks to my sisters, Luanna Straker and Ronna Worrell, and brother Arturo Wilson for your unconditional love and support in all I do, including this book. Deacon Elisa Bracero, my sister and spiritual guide; Lorri Dyson, my sister, you always come through for me. Laura Nichols, you did not hesitate to help with the review even with less than 24 hours review time. Dalys Macon, Aleks Stefanovska, Yolanda Johnson, Kristen Kiefer, Dr. Melida Harris Barrow, Omozua Isiramen, Bodo J. Frost, Dr. David John St. Clair, Norma Hollis, Bill Stierle, and Jennie Ritchie: you are always just a phone call, Skype or Zoom video away whenever I need support, a few minutes, or a few hours. For each of you and all those I did not mention thank you and God Bless each of you always. You put up with every single insane request I sent your way.

And last but never least; I thank each of you for purchasing this book. I am humbled and honored to present this book to you, the reader. I pray that it serves you well and helps guide what you say and what you do to inspire your tribe. Best wishes on your leadership journey.

"The most powerful leadership tool you have is your own personal example."
- John Wooden

Table of Contents

FOREWORD
by Jan Fraser

"One woman is unsinkable. Women united are unstoppable." *
Jan Fraser

I met one woman, Ilka Chavez, in November 2015 at a business conference. The moment I met her, I knew she was unsinkable. She had a glow, an energy and a magnetism that could not be denied. We bonded instantly. During the event, we spoke about our goals for business and life.

She shared that besides seeking what was her next career or business move, she was in the midst of a tough health challenge and the beginnings of a marriage dissolution. As I continued to speak to Ilka, I realized that what I saw in her she could not see in herself.

I said, "Ilka, you are a dynamic public speaker and best-selling author. You just don't realize it yet!" She looked at me as though I had no idea what I was saying. I knew she would touch lives with her voice and generosity as a treasured motivational speaker and a best-selling author. I invited her to my home for a Writer's Retreat.

Ilka took the risk, trusted her gut and joined me at this retreat. I received confirmation that she was a writer. She simply did not know the messages she had hidden deep inside her.

I asked Ilka to be a part of our collaborative book entitled, *Success University for Women in Business*. She wrote her chapter on honoring your values where she shared her values; respect, integrity, generosity, humility, trust and servitude. I would add that I affectionately refer to Ilka as my 'gratitude sister.' She affectionately refers to me as her 'fairy godmother.' She has taught me how important it is to be constantly grateful. I can attest that Ilka lives by all the values she wrote about in our book.

I invited her to speak and motivate at my Success University for Women in Business Conference in Bermuda in April. She touched countless women with her message of leadership.

I know that "women united are unstoppable" * and we were united.

In *What Leaders Say and Do, How to Inspire Your Tribe*, she shares lessons and pointers for daily living. She has served in many leadership positions in government, politics, and in private industry and is well-respected in her field.

I am confident you will be impacted by the information in this book and it will help strengthen your leadership life.

Congratulations Ilka on following your passion to grow leaders through this book and the speaking events this book inspires.

Jan Fraser Coles
July 28, 2017

Jan is the very definition of a 'self-starter' bringing real world experience humor, energy and relevant stories to her keynotes, training and coaching for over 42 years. Her focus is sales and customer service success.

Jan is a Certified Canfield Advanced Senior Level Trainer and Professional Success Coach. She has authored six books and best sellers and is the Co-Founder of *Success University for Women* books and conferences.

www.janfraser.com
www.janfraserbusinesstraining.com

"True leadership is about inspiration.
It's about having a vision,
believing in that vision,
and being willing to sacrifice for that vision in a
way that inspires others to join you."
– Anna Maria Chávez, Former CEO
of Girl Scouts of the USA

Preface/Introduction

Luke 6:38 (NIV®)

"Give, and it will be given to you. A good measure, pressed down, shaken together, running over, will be poured into your lap. For with the measure you use, it will be measured to you."

I write this book because of the cry I see and hear from individuals searching for great leadership and the yearning to share my experience. I hear this desire for leadership not just from the upcoming generations, but also from the baby boomer generations. They are searching for great leaders to follow, how to become great leaders, how to be inspired and how to inspire others. These varied generations are seeking leadership and guidance and are uncomfortable looking at themselves as leaders because what they see is a double standard when it comes to model leadership. Namely, what they see in leadership is not what they want to become.

The phrase "transformational leadership" was coined by leadership expert James McGregor Burns in his 1978 book, *Leadership*. He defined the concept as a process where "leaders and their followers [future leaders] raise one another to higher levels of morality and motivation." As leaders, I wonder if straying too far from our morals and values is what enables us to stray far from confidence in our ability to lead.

Is it a raised awareness of morals, or is it motivation upcoming leaders seek? One of the areas that I am passionate about is returning to conscious leadership, starting with one's personal values as a leader. Has economics taken first place over values, morals, and ethics? This may be why there is such a loud cry for good leaders. The cry aligns with Mr. McGregor Burns' definition of transformational leadership. Maybe the cry is for leaders who transform themselves and others.

I believe that we are all leaders in our own right and that we should all learn to lead from where we are. We don't have to be the president or CEO of a company to lead something. I have watched families crumble due to parents failing to understand their roles as leaders of their families. I watched organizations crumble because of egos, and watched leaders lose their focus by making the organization's mission about them instead of their customers and their tribe (their team or those they lead). Bottom line, it became not about the mission of the organization but about "what is in it for me." The 'lost leaders' strayed from their core values to seek worldly possessions and selfish desires. This happened in my own family and in several organizations where I served as a leader. I dug deep and realized that as leaders we must be transparent, vulnerable, and speak the truth. It has never been truer that a leader must calibrate his or her own compass before she can guide others.

Another lesson I learned from my experiences is that until you inspire yourself, you are truly unable to inspire others. Inspiration and empowerment in my eyes are the same. If you are a leader and you don't feel empowered, it is a very difficult task to empower others when you haven't gone through the requisite process to reach that state. This is exactly what I referred to earlier that leading others begins with leading yourself. You are not able to inspire and empower others if you focus only on yourself, or on "what is in it for me" (WIIFM) rather than what is in it for everyone.

Being elected as a leader is an honor that comes with great responsibility. We must carry many burdens that come with the union of different people and backgrounds. Embracing that diversity is not an easy task. As leaders, we must recognize our human ego. Change affects us as much as our teams and we must be constantly vigilant. A key aspect that we must pay attention to is what we say and how we act–always. As a society and as leaders, we need to awaken to the leader within and lead ourselves first, instead of leading others first and leaving the leftovers or nothing for ourselves.

In my own life, I was so busy leading in the corporate world, in my community, and within my family, that I completely forgot about me. As I woke up from my trance of serving so many–I was a "walking dead person", a people pleaser–I realized I had simply forgotten to include myself on the list of priorities.

No time equals no priorities.

We often forget that our children/our teams are looking for guidance from us and that our tribe relies on us to help them grow.

About a year ago, I partnered with two colleagues in the coaching business, Norma Hollis and William Stierle to host a conference entitled: *What leaders say and do: how to inspire your tribe*. The focus of this conference was to educate leaders of all levels on three key things we thought were important for leading your tribe. The three key areas are authenticity, communication, and leadership. Authentic leaders are not afraid to cry or show vulnerability; they are not afraid to tell the team "I do not know the answer"; they are not afraid to tell the team about their weaknesses and areas in which they need to grow; and, simply, they show up authentically every single time. Being authentic brings peace of mind. You wear no masks and can be who you are with all your imperfections. You are showing your team that, although you are their leader, we all have imperfections and areas where we need to grow or where we can improve. Authenticity means always speaking the truth. You do not have to tell a lie to impress others or make yourself look superior.

The next area I chose to focus on for this conference was communication. As leaders, we must understand that we all have different styles of communication. When we take the time to understand the way we communicate and, most importantly, the way each member of our tribe communicates, we are better able to harmonize our relationships with and between our tribes. As a bonus, we took it a step further and discussed *why* we communicate. Understanding the purpose behind an individual expressing a message in addition to understanding the way they convey said message was a true eye opener for those attending the conference as it highlighted the significance and power of communication not solely in business, but in life.

The third focus was on leadership. Understanding why your tribe follows you is important. What are the things you say and do which inspire your tribe to remain loyal and obedient? Why are leadership and leadership styles so important currently? How can we continuously improve as leaders?

This book was birthed from that conference. I wanted to write about what leaders say and do to inspire their tribes. I also thought the book could serve as a guide and as a reminder of some of the great historical leaders, how they inspired their tribes, and how they changed themselves to keep people inspired.

This book is written to enlighten new leaders and leaders-in-transition on key elements to help them be great leaders who inspire their current team, and ultimately the tribe they gather over time. I also hope this book serves as a reminder that, as leaders, you must continually work on improving yourself. If you are not pruning what no longer serves you, if you are not continuously working on improving your relationships, then your leadership will falter; you will be stuck, and you will stunt your growth and that of your tribe.

As leaders, you must be accountable and own this honor to lead with pride. You must inspire others to grow, not to die. When your tribe and those seeking your guidance or leadership see that you are human as they are, you inspire them to be confident. Leaders get sick, make mistakes, get tired, or lose their true north just like everyone else. Anchor yourself in your values and your words will inspire your tribe!

The *Maxwell Leadership Bible*[4] talks about how, as parents, we are called to lead our children. "If we start off a child in the way they should go, when they are old they will not turn from it." (Proverbs 22:6.) In his book, Maxwell posed the question, "How does a parent become a good leader for a child?" The answer provided in the book resonates closely with my belief and what I have done in leading my family and teams. I believe in being a great example and showing how, not telling, what to do. There is no excuse not to be a good example. Using your past as an excuse is not acceptable. 'Do as I say not as I do' is not a way of handling things that would inspire anyone.

We must be courageous leaders for our children's sake. We must manage and know the strengths of each of our children to best lead them. Have fun and create lasting moments. The sweet memories of my childhood, the fun times we had as a family, the lessons I learned about being stronger together than apart I learned from spending quality time with my family. I have long used these memories as a guide to lead my own family and leading my teams, my tribes.

Maxwell provides the following three answers on how to become a good leader for a child:

1. Modeling: He quotes Abraham Lincoln: "There is but one way to train up a child in the way he should go, and that is to travel it yourself." Maxwell further elaborates on the importance of a good example: "What you do has more impact on your child than all the lectures you could ever give."[4]

2. "Management: Good management is the ability to discern the uniqueness of a child and teach him or her accordingly. We are to train up a child in the way he should go. It is important to remember that different individuals have different destinies. This may mean we will have to adapt our styles, depending on the child's temperament and wiring."[4] Unfortunately, school systems can't do this for our children with their standardized way of educating. As a former school board member, I struggled with the idea of standardizing anything.

Each child is unique, yet our teachers and school systems are in shackles and chains because they are not given the flexibility and creativity to adapt to every child that presents in the classroom. Instead, I feel that teachers are forced to adapt the child to the system rather than the system to the child. This seems like a critical area that may cause some of the struggles in our school systems. I believe all children have the capacity to learn just as I believe all people have the capacity to lead. However, as Maxwell states, it requires adapting our styles to each different child. This is one reason I believe leading is more like a chess game than like checkers. Checkers is game where all the pieces move in the same direction. In chess, you move each chess piece in a different direction to maximize the ability of each chess piece to win the game. Chess requires more strategic thinking. For me, the more I grow and help others grow I think about playing chess rather than checkers. I hope as leaders we will do what is right for all our children or those following our lead.

3. Memories: Parents should create memories. Why? Because memories are more important than things."Note that the verse says, 'when they are old, they will not turn…' This implies that the child retains some memories of early experiences and embraces them later in life."[4] I am a true witness to this. It all comes full circle: Demonstrate what you expect; manage and encourage the individuals based on those expectations; create memories to generate an attachment and devotion to carrying on your goals as a leader. This can also easily apply to the things you do to inspire your tribe.

I hope this book serves to inspire you as a leader, yes you! In "my book" everyone is a leader.

*"Leaders become great,
not because of their power,
but because of their ability to empower others."
– John Maxwell*

Chapter One:
What is Leadership? Why is Leadership so Important?

2 Corinthians 9:6-8 (NIV)

"Remember this: Whoever sows sparingly will also reap sparingly, and whoever sows generously will also reap generously. [7] Each of you should give what you have decided in your heart to give, not reluctantly or under compulsion, for God loves a cheerful giver. [8] And God is able to bless you abundantly, so that in all things at all times, having all that you need, you will abound in every good work."

Let's look at some familiar depictions of leadership:

- The office or position of **a leader** by title
- A person with the capacity to **lead**
- The act or an instance of thought-**leading**
- The action of **leading** a group of people or an organization

Contrarily, my definition of leadership is aligning your values with your actions, words, and the way you live and inspiring others to do the same to make the workplace and the world a better place.

Now, let's look at how some of the great leaders define leadership:

- "Leadership is influence – nothing more, nothing less."
  – John Maxwell, leadership expert
- "If your actions create a legacy that inspires others to dream more, learn more, do more and become more, then, you are an excellent leader." – Dolly Parton, singer
- "Leadership is a series of behaviors rather than a role for heroes."
  – Margaret Wheatley, writer and management consultant

- "Good leaders organize and align people around what the team needs to do. Great leaders motivate and inspire people with why they're doing it. That's purpose. And that's the key to achieving something truly transformational."
  –Marilyn Hewson, Lockheed Martin Chairman, President and CEO
- "Ninety percent of leadership is the ability to communicate something people want." – Dianne Feinstein, U.S. Senator
- "Presenting leadership as a list of carefully defined qualities (like strategic, analytical and performance-oriented) no longer holds. Instead, true leadership stems from individuality that is honestly and sometimes imperfectly expressed…Leaders should strive for authenticity over perfection." – Sheryl Sandberg, Facebook COO
- "A leader is best when people barely know he exists, when his work is done, his aim fulfilled, they will say: we did it ourselves." – Lao Tzu, Chinese philosopher
- "Leadership is the capacity to translate vision into reality."
  – Warren Bennis, scholar and organizational consultant
- "The challenge of leadership is to be strong, but not rude; be kind, but not weak; be bold, but not bully; be thoughtful, but not lazy; be humble, but not timid; be proud, but not arrogant; have humor, but without folly." – Jim Rohn, author and motivational speaker

It is apparent that people who hold traditional positions of leadership all define leadership in different ways. Defining leadership only touches on the surface of its importance. As a mother, I am called to lead my children in the way they should lead their own lives. My role is to lead by the best example that I know. I define my values, then lead and live by my values. Values are key to leadership as these are the things you are not willing to compromise—the things you hold near and dear to who you are. My values are respect, integrity, generosity, humility, trust, and servitude. These are the principles that define my leadership and the choices I make when leading and influencing others.

Leadership is also important because the leader creates the vision, then helps others identify how and where they can lead using their strengths to attain the vision. Leaders are skillful in empowering others. How do you empower others as a leader? I will discuss this further in the section about what leaders do. Having a clear understanding of leadership is key as you lead your tribe. As a leader, one must also understand and know how to follow. For me as a leader, a core lesson in understanding leadership is to know that you don't always have to be ahead or pushing from behind. We can lead by walking side by side with our tribe. We all learn and grow from each other. The reassurance is in knowing that you are not walking by yourself, but that you have an entire team with varied skills and abilities to help fulfill your mission. Leadership is not an individual sport; it is a team sport. By this, I mean that every member is responsible and accountable for the role they play on the team.

As leaders, it is important to stay in your lane. You hire a team to help you build or attain a certain mission and vision. We must trust our team members and hold them accountable to do their part as part of the team. For example, you may hire a general contractor to build a home for you. That general contractor may have in-depth knowledge of all the necessary steps and resources needed to build a sturdy home. However, he doesn't necessarily possess every expertise that is needed to build your home. He may subcontract with companies that possess certain expertise to ensure a quality product is delivered. Some experts may be a carpenter who understands the intricate details of carpentry, or a painter who understands what type of paint to utilize for different surfaces. The contractor may also have someone who specializes in roofing. The point here is that as leaders we cannot know or be experts in every single area needed to accomplish our mission and or vision. The key to leadership is knowing how to orchestrate the larger vision of the work to be completed and simply harmonizing all the instruments to create beautiful, metaphorical music. You don't need to know how to play all the instruments, but you do need to know when to introduce each instrument into the concert.

In the next chapter, I will discuss some of the things that leaders say to inspire their tribe and teammates. To be chosen to lead others is a privilege and an honor that should never be taken for granted. Whether you are chosen to lead a country, a fortune 500 company, your family, or yourself, it is an opportunity to influence and inspire others and an opportunity to teach with your actions and words.

As noted in a Deloitte University Press article entitled "Leadership Awakened, Generations, Teams, and Science," leadership is a growing concern among business leaders.[9] The expanding age of the workforce, increase in group productivity, and fast pace of change brought on by overwhelming technology create constant challenges for people in leadership.

"Organizations need to refocus on leadership to build versatile leaders earlier in their careers, form leadership teams that mix different generations and varieties of leaders, and develop leaders deeper in the organization—all with a structured and evidence-based foundation for leadership priorities, programs, and investments.

- The leadership challenge is urgent and growing in importance. In 2016, 89 percent of companies see leadership as an important or very important issue (up from 87 percent in 2015), and 57 percent cite leadership as very important (up from 50 percent).
- Twenty-eight percent of respondents reported weak or very weak leadership pipelines.
- The profile for top leaders is complex and evolving. Organizations need to develop fundamental leadership capabilities among critical individuals and teams—capabilities that include the ability to collaborate across boundaries,

conceptualize new solutions, motivate diverse teams, and develop the next generation of diverse and global leaders."[9]

Leading and inspiring others is like a game of chess. It requires deep thought and strategy, and one bad move can ruin your game. It requires commitment and focus on all the pieces on the board. Have you thought of all the members of your tribe as a chess piece? Each piece, each move is critical in accomplishing the mission. No piece is less important that the other.

In the book *Chess Not Checkers: Elevate Your Leadership Game*[6], Mark Miller discusses how the first move you make in chess is to diligently move your chess pieces into position to maximize their impact. "You can't wait until you need a leader to start developing one."[6] Just like strategy in a chess game, you should start developing your leaders from the time they join your tribe, regardless of their position in the organization. As leaders, we must create a leadership mindset where every team player sees themselves as leading the work for which they are accountable. No one job is more important than the other; each position is critical to ensure that the organization runs smoothly. As I said to teams I have led, "The conductor is not more important than the engineer." They all must constantly communicate and work in harmony to ensure the train moves smoothly, arrives safely to the next stop, and securely delivers all passengers.

Miller also said in his book that, "your capacity to grow leaders depends on your ability to lead."[6] Growing and inspiring your tribe to lead from where they are is critical in sustaining a great organization. Surviving and winning the game of chess depends on your moves. It is the same with leadership—what you say and what you do determines if you win over or lose your tribe. It defines and measures the health of your organization.

Many people think they are not leaders because their role or position doesn't have a customary "leadership" title. John C. Maxwell said it best in *Maxwell's Leadership Bible*. He states, "If you are a parent, a teacher, a day care provider, a pastor, a coach—you are leading others all the time."[4]It doesn't matter your career or your role in your family. You are always leading and influencing someone or something.

Maxwell also emphasizes the "inside out" strategy to leadership which I subscribe to; you must start with "you." He states, "You and I were created to lead, to 'rule over the earth' (Genesis 1:26, 28). But as sinful beings, we tend to go our own way instead of following God's leadership."[4] We are frequently hard-headed and do what we feel like doing, trying to control everything despite the impossibility of controlling everything. I ask you to look in the mirror and have an honest conversation with yourself about how you are leading others. If it doesn't start with leading yourself, you might consider taking steps to improve the way you lead others. I don't mean any disrespect by this statement; I simply have experienced this myself and I am on a mission to help other leaders awaken. We matter, but our tribe matters more—they will be leading our legacy.

As a coach and one who encourages others to awaken their potential, I believe that our leadership begins from the inside out. We must know who we truly are to be able to lead others. When we try to be like others and not who we were made to be, we falter and sometimes lead our entire tribes, or even countries, down a ditch.

As leaders, you must do the hard work in finding who you are as you lead others. This is one reason that today's society craves purpose, mastery, and independence. The way to learn this is to understand what drives us to lead others and ourselves. *Drive*, the #1 New York Times bestselling book by Daniel Pink, suggests that the source of human motivation and our best work comes from our inherent drive towards autonomy, mastery, and purpose.[8] Many people struggle to find their purposes and therefore lose motivation at some point in their lives or careers. They travel life's journey oblivious to their call as leaders. For some, it takes decades to find their true purpose. For me, it took three decades to awaken to my purpose in life of growing leaders at all levels.

As I reflect on my life and career, no matter what I did I was always identified as a leader or asked to lead. With family, at work, and in my community, I somehow always managed to bubble up to the top and either personally volunteered or was "voluntold." Although my personal preference was always to lead from behind the curtains, I was not destined to travel that road. I awakened to the reality that I have a servant-leader's heart and found joy in serving others no matter the task assigned to me. I never looked at the "ask" as the leader. In other words, all I wanted was to accomplish what was asked of me to the best of my ability. I was simply one piece of the puzzle and the puzzle would not be complete if I didn't do my part. Sometimes, I found myself holding many pieces of the puzzle. As a leader, you will find that sometimes puzzle pieces are poured onto your desk. Your task is to figure out which pieces are yours and which you need to hand over to the right people with the proper expertise to ensure the puzzle is completed timely and to specification.

"In this world, you're either growing or you're dying
so get in motion and grow."
–Lou Holtz

Notes/Reflection

Why is leadership important to you? What are some of your daily leadership practices?

Notes/Reflection

Chapter Two:
What Leaders Say to Inspire Their Tribe

Galatians 6:6-10 (ESV)

"One who is taught the word must share all good things with the one who teaches. Do not be deceived: God is not mocked, for whatever one sows, that will he also reap. For the one who sows to his own flesh will from the flesh reap corruption, but the one who sows to the Spirit will from the Spirit reap eternal life. And let us not grow weary of doing good, for in due season we will reap, if we do not give up. So then, as we have opportunity, let us do good to everyone, and especially to those who are of the household of faith."

As a leader, you must be conscious of the words you speak and the things you say to others. You may ask yourself "Why would it matter what I say?" What you say matters because your tribe is always listening for your words and thoughts to inspire them to keep going. They are seeking your guidance to ensure a good outcome for all. Whether you are a leader of a country, of a classroom, of your family, or just yourself, you must always be cognizant to speak words that are truth—those that bring life and shine light on the facts, not on your personal beliefs.

True leaders' actions are congruent with their words. As a leader, sometimes it is not necessary to speak one word because your actions speak louder than your words. Do you say to your tribe "follow me" or do you say "I will come with you?" Do you speak words that reflect servitude to your tribe or reinforce that you are the boss and they must listen and do as you say? The generation X-ers and millennials have little tolerance for being told what to do. However, as I work with more generation X-ers and millennials, I observe that they are more inspired by inclusion, respect, a heart of service, purpose, freedom to create, flexibility with work schedules, and following leaders who truly know their purpose.

Before I dive into the things some of the well-known world leaders have said to inspire their tribes, I remind you that **leadership starts with you**:

- What do you say to yourself?
- How do you lead and inspire yourself?
- Do you practice some type of morning routine of meditation, prayer, or a different practice to center yourself?

Leading yourself is one of the most important things that determine how you lead others. I encourage you to think about the things you say to yourself. Do you start your day with gratitude for all that you have, gratitude for your tribe, and gratitude for being chosen to lead others?

Healthy leadership equals healthy followership. If the leader is healthy, whole, and constantly checks in on his own mental, physical, and emotional stability, then he is better equipped to do the same for his tribe.

Leaders say, "Ask questions." One of the takeaways I had from attending Jack Canfield's "Breakthrough to Success" conference was when he said that one secret to success is "Ask, Ask, Ask." I interpreted what he said to indicate that we should keep asking questions until we figure out a solution or get an answer. Asking questions activates your thinking, and thinking activates your creativity and your tribe's creativity. You as the leader should also ask questions of yourself to ensure you are tapping into your inner creativity.

Some leaders choose to operate with an open-door policy; others feel stressed with such a policy. Having an open-door policy says to your tribe, "I am here for you, I have time for you."

As I learn (and I am still learning) to prioritize, I developed effective prioritization exercises. As I acquired these skills and tools through learning and teaching quality improvement, I realized that not having time was equivalent to not having priorities. This was a true 'aha' moment for someone who thought leading was taking care of others before oneself.

Think about this: you say you have no time to exercise but the day goes by and you spend hours on your cell phone, browsing through Facebook, checking on everybody else's life except your own. Next time you say to yourself there are not enough hours in the day, take a real look at how you spend every minute of your 24-hour day. I challenge you to go through a prioritization exercise to fix the problem. You will thank yourself and your tribe will thank you even more. I take the liberty to say this because these were mistakes I made. I realized, however, that I had to change.

Leaders admit their mistakes to their tribe. They don't blame their tribe for their mistakes. They take full accountability for all errors occurring within their tribe. They frequently go over lessons learned as a team and discuss ways to improve without admonishing one another. We are human first, leaders second. Teach others to learn from life lessons rather than sulk in regret. Life is about growing, not about winning or losing.

Leaders provide words of encouragement to their tribe. "I believe in you," "You can do it," "Do you want to work on the new project?," "Job well done," "Please," "Thank you," "I am proud of your accomplishments," "Let's celebrate reaching our goals…" These are just a few words of encouragement leaders should be naturally saying to their tribe asa part of your fabric as a leader.

In chapter 4, I provide a sample list of quotes that have helped inspire individuals, tribes, companies, and nations. My hope is that these quotes serve as a reminder that you, too, can inspire your tribe by what you say. I encourage you to remember the words from Proverbs 18:21: "The tongue has the power of life and death, and those who love it will eat its fruit." As a leader, it is important to check what you say and how you say it to ensure that your words are building up and not tearing down your tribe. I encourage you to define what you gain from tearing down another person with your words. What you say matters.

"Remember the difference between a boss and a leader;
a boss says 'Go!'
a leader says 'Let's go!'"
– E.M. Kelly

Notes/Reflection

What are some phrases you say to inspire your tribe? What are the phrases you currently say to your tribe that you would like to change? Think about how you would like to improve your communication to continue to inspire your tribe?

Chapter Three:
What Leaders Do to Inspire Their Tribe

Hebrews 13:7 (NIV)

"Remember your leaders, who spoke the word of God to you. Consider the outcome of their way of life and imitate their faith."

The most important thing a leader does to inspire their tribe is to "walk the talk" or show their tribe what they expect. They don't tell them what to do, they show them how. Great leaders also share their talents; they don't save them up for a rainy day or for themselves. They don't whine. They find an indomitable spirit and persevere during turbulence. They lift their tribe. They teach their tribe to work with their community instead of working to serve themselves. Are you a leader that focuses on what's in it for me (WIIFM) or what's in it for us (WIIFU)?

A true leader is never selfish nor tries to take all the credit for herself. Instead, she focuses on how everyone on the team can win or how best to ensure that all collaborative relationships are win-win. Leaders: your tribe is stronger together than apart. When you pit one against the other to entice competition, when all is said and done, no one wins and everyone loses. We were created to be in community: when one is down, the other members of the tribe can fill the gap. The same applies in terms of what leaders do—they understand the strength of each member of their tribe and ensure that they are placed in opportunities to exercise strengths yet still practice and improve on weaknesses.

One personal example of leadership started as I transitioned from a private consultant to a civil servant and from independence to bureaucracy. Can you imagine the adjustment? I made an agreement with myself that I would not sacrifice my work ethics or my values no matter how the bureaucracy operated.

I was laser focused on understanding how big government worked. I was interested in the operations. My thought was that if you know the inner function, then you can figure out the rest. During this transition, I decided to commute almost two hours each way to and from work to gain what I knew would be valuable experience. This position, although a long haul, would begin to equip me with the necessary experience and understanding on how big government worked. This position was in the then Health Care Financing Administration (HCFA) now Center for Medicare and Medicaid Services (CMS).I never intended to stay at this position very long because the commute was too far, I had a young daughter at home, and my husband traveled frequently.

I realized that the commute was too much when I nearly crashed one morning making the two-hour drive. I knew that was the sign to seek a different position. That very morning, I went into the office and gave my two-week notice. I realized I had reached my limit. Fortunately, my supervisors at the time valued my work and assisted me in finding a position closer to home. This was a great example of how leaders take care of their tribe.

A few weeks later, I was asked to interview with someone who was leading a new initiative and implementing a new legislation I knew nothing about. I interviewed for the position and shortly thereafter was offered the position. My learning curve was high, but I trusted that my foundational experience landed me the position and the rest would come. Short side-note, this new job led me to fly to the inauguration of this special initiative on my first day on the job. Long story short, my new supervisor was interviewed about the new initiative which I was still not clear about so I listened intently to learn. One reporter wanted an interview in Spanish and my supervisor looked at me and said, “She knows Spanish.” Can you imagine my panic? Well, I did the interview and the reporter seemed satisfied with the information I provided. My new supervisor looked at me and said, “You are hired.” Talk about taking on a leadership role. I had never interviewed with media in Spanish, the duties of the new position entailed something I never did before, and there I was jumping in as though I had experience.

I believe this started me on my path to understanding the importance of being prepared to lead and reinvent yourself(and preparing your team to reinvent)and lead themselves as initiatives come and go with different administrations or changes in general. In government, when you are working with one administration, you may be working on one hot topic and the next administration something not so hot. This relates to all aspects of life, however, not just government. When we have a change in power, health, life, structure, or any other variety of ways things changes every day, it is how we handle that change that makes us great leaders.

Since learning this lesson, I tried to encourage all those in my many tribes to constantly do the work to stay aware, remain nimble, flexible, and always be prepared to grow.

Leaders plan and prepare for the worst. Things may not always go as planned but the mission must continue. Members of your tribe may decide to leave the tribe to continue growing their career or for other reasons. Preparing your team for many of these unexpected events is critical. Sometimes as leaders we forget that succession planning is important and we rely on a sole expert to do the important work. When that expert leaves the tribe, and sometimes the leader, acts as though the world is coming to an end. This I believe happens because as a society we become stagnant. We get so caught upin routine and forget that we must continuously work on improving ourselves, and train our tribes to keep up with the most current tools and information to progress as an organization.

Another key aspect to leadership is to set realistic expectations for yourself and your tribe. Otherwise, disappointment will quickly infiltrate your tribe and cause resentment. Then you, as the leader, are spending time cleaning up the mess caused by setting unrealistic expectations or having no expectations set at all. Many leaders will read this and say, "I at least set clear expectations." But do you really?

I, too, as leader said the same thing and clearly missed the mark. Earlier in my career, as a leader of a small team, I was given an assignment when my plate was already filled. Instead of speaking up, I took on one more assignment that left me working unsurmountable hours that caused me to miss my children's after school activities. I became resentful that I had to work into the evening hours without extra compensation instead of being home enjoying seeing my children grow. Now that I have more experience, I take full responsibility for not setting realistic expectations and for not telling my supervisor that my plate was already full and that we needed to discuss prioritization of my assignments. Clearly in this situation, I fell short of my charge as a leader.

Please think and ask your tribe early and often if your expectations and instructions are clear. If they understand the task and have the right tools, you should still check in to ensure they are able to manage the task. Sometimes members of your tribe are struggling, yet are afraid to show their vulnerabilities. But if you develop an open and honest relationship with your tribe, you will be able to prevent lots of headaches. Distractions and diversions will interrupt the day-to-day grind, but the best investment of your time is in your tribe. As leaders, never forget you carry more power as a unit than as an individual. Part of your job is to inspire action by your tribe.

This brings us to a third key facet of leadership, which is completing the puzzle. You say to your team, "I have this puzzle to complete and I truly need your help." You first look to identify and define your role. I call this "observation." You then closely evaluate and understand the task at hand. One of my former and dear supervisors referred to this as knowing what is your "it." This comprises of the core of the assignment, the significant pieces.

Next, you "interpret" the assignment to really understand what it means—what is the purpose for accomplishing each part and ultimately the end goal? This helps ensure that I as the leader am clear about what things should look like and most importantly confirm that the team understands what the final product should look like.

Finally, you "correlate" or see if we have done any similar projects to avoid reinventing the wheel. If we have done similar puzzles, I pull the lessons learned and consider what worked well and what didn't work so well. If what worked well can be used to complete this puzzle then we can apply that lesson or tool to the new puzzle. Once all these pieces are gathered, I distribute the puzzle pieces to the appropriate team members with the plan and appropriate timeline or dates for deliverables. The above puzzle completion example is a sample of what leaders do and the steps I take as a leader.

One of the biggest hurdles to inspire our tribes as leaders is the hesitation to be vulnerable. A dear friend loaned me a book by Dr. Brené Brown after she met me for the second time. This book discussed how the courage to be vulnerable transforms the way we live, love, parent, and lead. Dr. Brown explained that the title of her book, *Daring Greatly*[1], is a phrase dubbed by Theodore Roosevelt's speech "Citizenship in a Republic." She proceeds to recount that speech, which is sometimes referred to as "The Man in the Arena." Dr. Brown, sounding almost awakened by the quote, said in her book, "This is vulnerability. Everything I've learned from over a decade of research on vulnerability has taught me this exact lesson. Vulnerability is not knowing victory or defeat, it's understanding the necessity of both; it's engaging. It's being all in."[1]

Dr. Brown shared the famous passage from Theodore Roosevelt's speech at the Sorbonne in Paris, France, on April 23, 1910. This passage awakened me so much, as I imagined it awakened Dr. Brown, that I decided to share in this section of the book:

> "It is not the critic who counts: not the man who points out how the strong man stumbles, or where the doer of deeds could have done them better.
>
> The credit belongs to the man who is in the arena, whose face is marred by dust and sweat and blood; who strives valiantly; who errs, who comes short again and again,
>
> Because there is no effort without error and shortcoming; but who does strive to do the deeds; who knows great enthusiasm, the great devotions; who spends himself in a worthy cause; who at the best knows in the end the triumph of high achievement, and who at the worst, if he fails, at least fails while daring greatly…"[1]

As I read this I thought, "Wow, I am not alone in this." It is about engaging with the people you rely on to get the work done, the tribe that helps you achieve your fame, the tribe that wins you awards. It is about being all in with them. That is the type of leader I strive to be all the time. I approach every engagement as a win-win because when the members of my tribe win, I win. When they lose, I lose. To have this win-win relationship, you must lead authentically, transparently, and with the best interest of all stakeholders in mind. I would often say to my tribe at work, "If you get a bad evaluation that reflects on me as I am ultimately responsible for your success." Some understood my message right away, but for others it took a few years to get there.

Another key to leadership is to show your tribe that it doesn't matter if you succeed or fail; either way, you always learn something. Failure is a lie. Disappointment is a figment of our own imagination. We need to set expectations that, no matter the outcome, we always learn something new. The key is to keep daring greatly and not to give up. You always win, you either finish or you grow. I challenge each leader who reads this book to answer the following questions: Are you daring greatly? Are you exposing your vulnerability? What are some things you will do to continuously improve your leadership? I remind you that no matter your title—whether you are a housewife, a student, someone that hands out flyers, or the president of a company or country—you are a leader from where you stand.

"He who is not contented with what he has, would not be contented with what he would like to have."
–Socrates

Learn to appreciate your current tribe. Show them your appreciation and gratitude early and often. Stop complaining to others about your team or your tribe, and talk to them directly to foster genuine relationships.

There is no perfect person. You hired the person; you should know what strengths you saw in this person and areas where they need to improve. When they are not performing in areas you knew needed improvement and you have not provided the tools for improvement, you cannot expect a stellar performance. Stop fooling yourselves. These are mistakes I made as a leader.

As mentioned earlier, each member of the tribe learns and operates differently. We may have to adapt our patterns to the way they are wired to ensure the success of each team member. Play on their strengths.

Detours will be present and things will happen. As leaders, you must be prepared to pivot and prepare your tribe to do the same.

Leaders also prepare their tribe to reinvent themselves and reinvent the organization as the tide changes.

Leaders set specific, measurable, attainable, realistic, and timeline (SMART) expectations. They stand and walk the journey alongside the members of their tribe. My leadership motto is that if we are running a race together and you fall, I will turn around, pick you up, and bring you across the finish line. There is nothing in my book that says I win and you lose.

Another key aspect of leadership is being accountable for all actions. As leaders, we should not blame others for something we lead. We must take on the responsibility of the entire tribe. We cannot take on responsibility for some members and not others. They are all part of our tribe. As leaders, playing favorites injures your tribe. Would you rather work with a healthy or injured tribe?

Lastly, it is very important that leaders share their talents. They should not bury them where they serve no one any good. Scripture tells about the "Parable of the Talents" in Matthew 25:14-30 where a master who was going on travel entrusted his property to his servants. In accordance with each of their abilities, the master gave five talents to one servant, a second servant received two talents and the third servant received one talent. Eight talents were entrusted to three servants (each talent was a significant sum of money). Upon return from his lengthy travel, the master asked the three servants to account for the talents he entrusted to them. The first and the second servants explained that they each put their talents to work, and doubled the value of the property with which they were entrusted; each servant was rewarded. The third servant with one talent was afraid, hid his talent and did not put it to work. He was not rewarded. The moral of the story through this parable as it relates to leadership is that we should not store our talents for ourselves—we must pass them along to our tribes. Leaders who choose not to lead transparently and authentically are not only leading falsely, but they are also missing opportunities to leave a great legacy.

Notes/Reflection

What are your leadership traits and characteristics? What actions will you take to continue to enhance your traits and characteristics?

Notes/Reflection

Chapter Four:
Great World Leaders' Quotes and Actions

"Everybody is a LEADER whether you know it or not. You oversee YOU and believe me, that is a full-time job! Leaders are those who claim their power to make things happen to benefit themselves and others."

– Mary Frances Winters

I chose five famous people who inspire me daily to keep growing as a leader. As I grow, as I lead my purpose, the things they did and said inspire me every day. Some are much younger than I and some are no longer with us. However, the one thing they all have in common is that they left or will leave a legacy of inspiration for hundreds, thousands and millions of people. They changed one life at a time. Here are prominent attributes these leaders possess(ed), things they said, and actions they took to inspire others, inspire their tribe, and inspire nations.

1. Abraham Lincoln - Life-long Learner, Connector, Charismatic

"To win a man to your cause, you must first reach his heart, the great high road to his reason."

President Lincoln was a story teller. He engaged through conversation, impacted individuals through discussion, public speaking and the gift of communication. He had great influence on others and was clearly a life-long learner. He put his country above himselfand focused on doing the right thing. One thing that I relate closely with Lincoln's leadership style is the ability to put himself in someone else's shoes first. Understand someone's 'why' first, then they can more easily understand your 'why.' All these characteristics prove to be from one who lived and loved to learn.

2. Malala Yousafzai- Courage, Humility, Compassion

"I am Malala," she said. "I am those 66 million girls who are deprived of education. And today I am not raising my voice. It is the voice of 66 million girls."

Malala at the tender age of 11 had the courage to begin a movement to advocate for education of children, especially girls deprived of education. She fought for a cause she believed in. She fought for others, not just herself. When she won the Nobel Peace Prize, she made her speech about 66 million girls around the world. She made her one voice resonate for 66 million voices. How powerful is that? One thing that I can relate to with Malala's leadership was her courage and to know at such a young age that the cause she pursued was not about her, it was about her tribe. That is the type of leadership I hope this book inspires. It is never about us, the leader. It is about the mission and those who help achieve that mission.

3. Dr. Martin Luther King, Jr. - Peace, Equality, Faith

"I have a dream that one day in Alabama little white boys and little white girls will be able to hold hands with little black boys and black girls as sisters and brothers."

Dr. King inspired a nation by standing up for what he believed without violence or disrespect. He truly fought for equality for all. His spiritual background help to strengthen his leadership and he frequently included scriptures from the Bible to deliver his message to the country and the world. His gift of communicating through his speeches inspired many people then and inspires me now. One thing I admire about Dr. King's leadership is how he relied on his strong faith to guide his leadership, and how he inspired many to have faith and persevere for the cause.

4. Eleanor Roosevelt - Honesty, Integrity, Strength

"It is not fair to ask of others what you are not willing to do yourself."

Eleanor Roosevelt was a woman who stood up for many causes. Her hardships gave her strength and courage. Despite sometimes having a grim present and future, she remained positive in her movement. Her positive outlook is one of the main traits that I admire about Mrs. Roosevelt. She also kept things honest and was a woman of integrity. I relate closely with this leadership trait. Honesty and integrity matter deeply to me as a leader. One thing I often say is that when I die, my integrity goes to the grave with me and leaves a legacy.

5. Mahatma Gandhi - Change Agent, Conscious, Servant Leader

Mahatma Gandhi inspired many by teaching people to lead through hope, faith, and love. In "Gandhi: The Man, "Eknath Easwaran wrote that Gandhi's recipe for success lied within his vision. Among all of the challenges he faced, he saw occasions in which he could serve others.

One thing that strikes me about Gandhi's leadership example was that failure and success depends on how you handle difficulties. He personally inspired me not to look at anything as a failure. You can always learn something from any endeavor you embark on that doesn't go exactly the way you want it to go. Sometimes that one thing that you or someone labels as failure is the thing that propels you to your next level.

Just as we have leaders that inspire, we have leaders who deflate others from growing to their full potential or from finding their purpose in life. I encourage each of you to inspire your tribe to find their 'why' (purpose) or their 'what' (where they belong). Show them through your actions and word show to achieve their greater potential and live their life's purpose.

Continue working on yourself while you inspire others so you don't fall prey to what I call "hurt leaders, hurt their tribe." Leaders are sometimes like wounded warriors and continue to lead, despite their wounds. Sometimes those wounds bleed out onto their tribes. Dr. R. A. Vernon of the Word Church in Cleveland, Ohio said as leaders "we lead and we bleed" at the same time. But how can a wounded person continue to lead as they bleed? Is the blood they leave on their tribe causing more bad than good? As parent leaders, if you are hurt or wounded, have you paused to check your wounds and ensure that you are not spilling the blood from your wounds onto your family, your tribe?

"We are what we repeatedly do.
Excellence, then, is not an act,
but a habit."
– Aristotle

Notes/Reflection

Start building your legacy. Write down your own quotes and why you believe they help inspire your tribe.

Chapter Five: Your Leadership Footprint

I ask all of you leaders to consider the following: What type of leader are you? Whether you are leading a fortune 500 company, your family, or yourself, what is the legacy you will leave? I have worked with many leaders who strive for perfectionism simply for self-benefit and not for the benefit of their tribe. Some leaders haven't even considered that their leadership is part of their footprint. I raise this topic to awaken you to the importance of your choices as a leader. If you are leading a tribe or your family, having perspective is important.

As the leader, you hold the vision before your tribe embraces that vision. You start with the end in mind. Successfully on boarding your tribe to that vision, a.k.a. 'the bus,' and keeping them on the bus or realizing that it is time for tribe members to exit the bus, will define your footprint.

Are you paying attention to your leadership footprint? Are you demanding excellence or perfection from your tribe? Most importantly, are you demanding excellence or perfection from yourself? It all starts with you.

What your tribe says and does both depends and reflects strongly on your actions, words and character. Are you working to the best of your ability to act, speak, and lead with respect, integrity, generosity, humility, trust, and servitude? As a leader it is critical to focus on continuously improving yourself and your skills, and equipping your team to do the same. This is essential for personal, professional, and spiritual growth.

If you seek perfection, you will miss the mark. Seeking excellence gives you a better chance of success. Do your best. My over three decades of experience in leadership positions has taught me that leadership requires grit and indomitable spirit. These traits allow you to take the lead on your life knowing that your strength comes from within. You are a leader from where you stand. You don't have to be the President of the company or the CEO to lead.

Grit, indomitable spirit, and perseverance will set you apart from the rest. No one can grow your greatness but you! Once you possess these characteristics, you can inspire your tribe to grow their greatness. When you feel that you can't lead, I encourage you to dig deep inside yourself and let your indomitable spirit push you beyond your mental and physical capacity. It is the key to running a marathon and finishing the race.

"Pursuing excellence unlike perfectionism...does not demand a sacrifice of self-esteem as it tends to focus on the process of achievement rather than outcome."
- Monica A. Frank, Ph.D.

There is a poem that I keep nearby to remind me to focus on excellence and not perfection as I continue my leadership journey. I believe this poem, author unknown, brings deep wisdom to each of us as leaders. I hope it serves you well as you continue your leadership journey to inspire your tribe by what you say and what you do.

Perfection vs. Excellence
Author Unknown

Perfection is being right.
Excellence is being willing to be wrong.
Perfection is fear.
Excellence is taking a risk.
Perfection is anger and frustration.
Excellence is powerful.
Perfection is control.
Excellence is spontaneous.
Perfection is judgment.
Excellence is accepting.
Perfection is taking.
Excellence is giving.
Perfection is doubt.
Excellence is confidence.
Perfection is pressure.
Excellence is natural.
Perfection is the destination.
Excellence is the journey.

"Try to become not a man of success, but try rather to become a man of value."
–Albert Einstein

Notes/Reflection

Have you thought about your leadership footprint/your legacy and what it looks like? How will you know and determine you are successful in leaving your footprint/leaving your legacy? Write your thoughts here.

Notes/Reflection

Chapter Six: Traits and Characteristics of Great Leadership

Great leaders demonstrate certain characteristics. The following attributes are ones I look for to determine whether the leaders I work with are those I should follow.

Great leaders are visionary. They see and communicate the big picture frequently. They also incorporate ways to keep the vision alive.

Great leaders are passionate about their work. They enjoy why and what they are doing and share this passion with their tribe. Even when it takes the tribe sometime to catch on to the vision, they find a way to keep the train moving in the right direction until the team is equipped or recognizes to the vision.

Great leaders always lead with integrity. They are open and transparent. They never throw their tribe under the bus. Instead, they would jump in front of the bus to save a member of their tribe (this is a figure of speech not literal).Every time you go to bat for your team, you teach integrity and honesty.

Great leaders start with trust and build it up even more along the way. They start all relationships with honest and reliable working relationships. They give each member of their tribe respect and trust. They give all the benefit of the doubt.

Great leaders are innovators, risk takers, and re-invention specialists that enable growth of tribe members. Without innovation, creativity, and ingenuity we remain the same as a tribe and don't develop and grow. If we don't keep looking for new and improved ways to grow as a tribe, we remain stuck. Yes, growth can sometimes become uncomfortable but it is necessary to keep thriving.

“If we’re growing, we’re always going to be out of our comfort zone. – John Maxwell

Great leaders ask great questions of their tribe, ask questions of themselves, and prioritize self-care. They look for the missing links in order to connect the dots, and they inspire through storytelling and sharing their experiences. In addition, they develop good habits such as exercising frequently, meditating, resting, reading, and in general investing time in their self-improvement and growth.

Great leaders develop a following by challenging, inspiring, and motivating every member of their tribe. They have a natural indomitable spirit—perseverance is in their blood—and they are continuously building their character and the character of their tribe members. Lastly, and perhaps most importantly, great leaders build hope.

Chapter Seven: Conclusion

As leaders, we must remain conscious of the impact of what we say and do to and in front of our tribe. Our work is to inspire others to be the change and to teach them to lead from where they are. It is not necessary to be President of a country or organization to lead an effort. Take Malala for example, she led a huge initiative at 11 years old from where she was– a student in hardship. She almost lost her life for this cause. She, however, believed so deeply in equal education rights for girls and all children that she was willing to sacrifice her life so that over 66,000 lives would have a voice. She recognized that her one voice could echo for 66,000 lives.

No matter where you are on the leadership chain, continue to grow, continue to learn, and continue to have courage. If you can't find the right leader, become the leader. Simply be the change you want to see by walking, talking, and acting in a manner that inspires you and your tribe. You are here to make a difference.

In summary, the following are things to keep in mind as you ponder what leaders say and do:

Listens -Distills what is important; "A wise man is hungry for truth while the dumb person feeds on trash." (Proverbs 15:14).

Engages - Pushes their tribe to the next level through constant communication and conversation

Accountable- Takes responsibility and follows through

Dependable and decisive

Empowers those in their tribe

Resilient and results-oriented

I would love to hear your thoughts and comments or if this book helped you in any way. If you'd like more information about the author or leadership training programs, please check out my website at www.corporate-gold.com or email me at WLSADIVC@gmail.com.

BONUS POCKET GUIDE

Ilka's pocket guide to inspiring others and leading in excellence daily.

1- Start your day with gratitude. For example, start a gratitude jar where you write the things that you are grateful for daily.
2- You can't inspire others if you haven't inspired yourself first. For example, many of us continue to battle with achieving a goal like weight loss. Eating healthier, being intentional about moving and exercising consistently and yielding results will inspire you. Others seeing your results will inspire them.
3- You can't empower others, without feeling empowered yourself.
4- Know your values. I encourage everyone to write down their values. I have memorized my values. They are respect, integrity, generosity, humility, trust and servitude. What are yours? Feel free to share these with me.
5- Honor and anchor your values…like your life depends on it. In the previous point, I encourage you to define your values. Now that you know your values, I encourage you to honor those values and let those values serve as your daily compass in making decisions.
6- Aim for excellence daily…show-up as the best "You." Bring your best effort in everything that you do. Do everything with integrity, respect and for the right reason.
7- Be inspired by other leaders, but don't become a copycat. You can always model the characteristics of others, however, please remember you are original and there is only one of you. You cannot be anyone else and no one can be you.
8- Become best friends with change, as that is the only constant in your life. Learn to embrace change. Learn that change is not a

bad thing. When change shows up, good or bad, it means you are growing. Growth is a good thing.

9- 'Flip Da Script' every time. Instead of saying "I failed," say "what have I learned?" Isn't learning more fun than failing?
10- Learn your lesson, forgive, let go and keep moving forward. As you grow, don't harbor resentment or anger. It does you no good.
11- Be always prepared for growth and shifts…Continuous improvement is key. As leaders, it is critical to pause during the leadership journey to reflect on the things that are working well, the things that need improvement, and things that we may need to stop doing. This is critical to ensure you continue to grow individually and as a tribe.
12- Always be prepared for conflict. I add this because the question is not "if" but "when" conflict arrives. Will you be prepared? Will you be on the offensive or defensive team?
13- Learn how to stand strong in conflict. I share this because some may think that because someone throws the punch first they must punch back. However, many of my victories were won by responding in kindness, with respect, in integrity and sometimes simply by remaining silent and keeping my hands to my side.
14- Find what inspires you most and pass it on. As I continue to grow into my purpose, I find that I truly enjoy what I do and sharing all that I know with others. It never feels like work. Find your purpose and freely share your knowledge and wisdom with many. That will be part of your legacy. Do not keep your talents to yourself.
15- Learn the lessons, teach the lessons, then lead the lessons. I share my many bumps in the road with my mentees as they will have their own bumps in the road to handle.
16- Never compromise your values. This is where integrity plays a crucial role.
17- You can't explain irrational so let it go! Many times, we try to rationalize our position with others. We simply must learn to live

with the fact that part of being human is that we have different point of views. It makes us stronger to live and work with others with different perspectives than our own.

18- Learn to make lemonade when life hands you lemons, and don't forget, it must be a much-improved batch of lemonade than the last. I say this kidding, however, everyone including leaders will have hard falls or things will not always go as planned. When that happens, learn what you must learn and continue moving forward and improving who you are.

19- Find activities that keep you awake. Don't become the walking dead. Don't get stuck in the routine. Pay attention and intentionally change your pattern so things remain new and fresh. The mundane sometimes puts us in a trance.

20- Search for your purpose if you haven't yet found it - seek your indomitable spirit and lead it! Keep working towards finding your true purpose. When you run into that "unhappy place," you know you have yet to find your purpose and your peace. Keep searching until you reach your goal.

His master replied,
'Well done, good and faithful servant! You have been faithful with a few things; I will put you in charge of many things. Come and share your master's happiness!"
–Matthew 25:23 (NIV)

REFERENCES

1. Brown, B. (2012). Daring Greatly. New York, New York: Gotham Books.
2. Economy, P. (2014, August 22). 17 Things Every Successful Leader Says Every Day. *Inc.* Retrieved from https://www.inc.com/peter-economy/17-things-every-successful-leader-says-every-day.html.
3. Maxwell, J. (1998). The 21 Irrefutable Laws of Leadership. Nashville, Tennessee: Thomas Nelson.
4. Maxwell, J. (2003). The Maxwell Leadership Bible -Lessons in Leadership from the Word of God. Nashville, Tennessee: Thomas Nelson.
5. McBean, B., Stuart, D., Nordstorm, T. (2013, January, 24). The 5 Characteristics of Great Leaders. *Fast Company.* Retrieved from https://www.fastcompany.com/3004914/5-characteristics-great-leaders.
6. Miller, M. (2015). Chess not Checkers: Elevate Your Leadership Game. Oakland, California: Berrett-Koehler Publishers.
7. Nayar, V. (2013, August 2). The Three Differences Between Managers and Leaders. Retrieved from https://hbr.org/2013/08/tests-of-a-leadership-transiti.html
8. Pink, D. (2011). Drive. New York, New York: Riverhead Books.
9. Wakefield, N., Abbatiello A., Agarwal D., Pastakia K., van Berkel A. (2016, February 29). Leadership Awakened - Generations, Teams, Science. *Deloitte University Press*. Retrieved from https://dupress.deloitte.com/dup-us-en/focus/human-capital-trends/2016/identifying-future-business-leaders-leadership.html.

TESTIMONIALS

"As expected, Ilka Chavez not only met but exceeded my expectations on her first book! Ilka lives by example and as part of her tribe I often benefit from her inspirations. WHAT LEADERS SAY AND DO is brilliantly filled with nuggets that build from the ground up and from the inside out. Ilka nails it by inspiring and encouraging all to know that you too are a LEADER, even if not leading a Fortune 500 company or family. She encourages all to LEAD in such manner that you leave a legacy not so much for ourselves but for generations to come. If you are looking to establish YOUR "leadership footprint," WHAT LEADERS SAY AND DO offers great tools to do so; a must read!" - Dalys Macon – Owner, Divine Order and IT Consultant

"Everyone can become a leader by following the inspirational and effective leadership model outlined in this book. The author highlights the necessary human traits and sound judgement to lead in both the work and home environment. It supports every leader's God Given Talent!"- Laura Nichols – Educational Leader

"I have led and mentored others in many areas at different times of my life. Every leader needs a leader and a mentor. Ilka is a leader and a mentor in my life. She encompasses everything that I believe about being a leader - vulnerability, resilience, empathy, consciousness, introspection, and seeing people past their faults. Success is found in making sure others succeed. This book and Ilka's character makes sure that others can succeed!!" Yolanda Johnson – Owner Beyond Measure, LLC (A leadership development company)

"Ilka Chavez reminds us that everyone is destined to be a leader at their own time. As you read the pages that follow, you too will be inspired by her courage to share her own journey and empowered by her contagious belief in growing leaders

and building greatness. Ms. Chavez knows exactly what leaders say and do because she is the epitome of excellence." Kristen Kiefer - Chief of Staff, National Council on Aging

"I met Ilka during the summer of 1997 and we have been friends/sisters ever since. As I read this authentically written book, I wondered why Ilka chose to use the word tribe instead of team. And then, I said - this is Ilka, her love, her servant heart has no limit. A team has limited members, and tribe does not. I feel privileged to be part of her tribe and I am loving how God is using her to reach many. Her obedience and dedication will earn her a well done -good and faithful servant from our Heavenly Father."-Elisa Bracero- Retired, Senior Leader United States Government and Deacon, Light of Life Church

"In a world of quick fixes, lack of patience and desire for fast-tracking career success, Ilka offers the truth about leadership. As a society, we have focused on climbing the corporate ladder that we have forgotten who we are and what our responsibilities are- to ourselves, to our kids and family, to our community, or our employers. We are more stressed and our benchmark for happiness keeps on moving. Ilka's book helps people who are serious about change. Because change is hard. And only those who really want it, will do the work needed to change habits. Note: not change the past or live with regret. Just change their habits so they can change their present and therefore the potential for the future.

Get the book. Read it. Apply it. Reap the rewards." – Aleks Stefanovska, College Admissions Coach and Founder, PainFreeToCollege.com

"As my deeply appreciated Vice President of Genius Actualizers, it is my honor to give this testimonial for a book so many have been waiting for. I know Ilka Chavez for a time that seems like ages. The first time I met her, I was in search for a special leadership expert for my World Awakening Summit. Ilka's charisma and radiance were instantly captivating. Her

integrity, purpose driven mission to inspire everyone she meets and every human being she naturally ignites with her "consistently walking the talk high values" immediately made her a great friend and tremendously trusted advisor. These impressions solidified even deeper during her certification journey with me to become an emotional mastery coach I certified with gratitude. Everyone choosing Ilka as a guide and leadership coach will make the experience to have made a decision that will satisfy long term. The book "What Leaders Say and Do" will leave you amped with inspiration, empowerment and the desire to learn more from her. I highly encourage you to connect with Ilka and experience elevation into your life and business."

-Dr. h.c. David John St Clair

Founder and President of Genius Actualizers NLP Trainer, Hypnotherapist, Author and Life/Executive Coach